BY ALLAN MOREY

THE SAN DIEGO
CHARGERS
STORY

BELLWETHER MEDIA · MINNEAPOLIS, MN

Are you ready to take it to the extreme? Torque books thrust you into the action-packed world of sports, vehicles, mystery, and adventure. These books may include dirt, smoke, fire, and chilling tales. **WARNING**: read at your own risk.

This edition first published in 2017 by Bellwether Media, Inc.

No part of this publication may be reproduced in whole or in part without written permission of the publisher. For information regarding permission, write to Bellwether Media, Inc., Attention: Permissions Department, 5357 Penn Avenue South, Minneapolis, MN 55419.

Library of Congress Cataloging-in-Publication Data

Names: Morey, Allan.
Title: The San Diego Chargers Story / by Allan Morey.
Description: Minneapolis, MN : Bellwether Media, Inc., 2017. | Series:
   Torque: NFL Teams | Includes bibliographical references and index.
Identifiers: LCCN 2015050795 | ISBN 9781626173804 (hardcover : alk. paper)
Subjects: LCSH: San Diego Chargers (Football team)–History–Juvenile literature.
Classification: LCC GV956.S29 M67 2017 | DDC 796.332/6409794985–dc23
LC record available at http://lccn.loc.gov/2015050795

Printed in the United States of America, North Mankato, MN.

TABLE OF CONTENTS

It is the last game of the 2013 season. The San Diego Chargers are up against the Kansas City Chiefs. With a win, the Chargers make the **playoffs**. With a loss, their season is over.

When the fourth quarter begins,
the Chargers are down by 10 points.
But they have the ball.

Eddie Royal

Quarterback Philip Rivers tosses a short pass to **wide receiver** Eddie Royal. Touchdown! The next time the Chargers have the ball, they kick a field goal. The score is now tied.

The game goes into overtime. The Chargers get the ball first. They go on to kick a field goal and win the game!

SCORING TERMS

END ZONE
the area at each end of a football field; a team scores by entering the opponent's end zone with the football.

EXTRA POINT
a score that occurs when a kicker kicks the ball between the opponent's goal posts after a touchdown is scored; 1 point.

FIELD GOAL
a score that occurs when a kicker kicks the ball between the opponent's goal posts; 3 points.

SAFETY
a score that occurs when a player on offense is tackled behind his own goal line; 2 points for defense.

TOUCHDOWN
a score that occurs when a team crosses into its opponent's end zone with the football; 6 points.

TWO-POINT CONVERSION
a score that occurs when a team crosses into its opponent's end zone with the football after scoring a touchdown; 2 points.

The San Diego Chargers have always had a high-powered **offense**. This has earned them the nickname "Super Chargers."

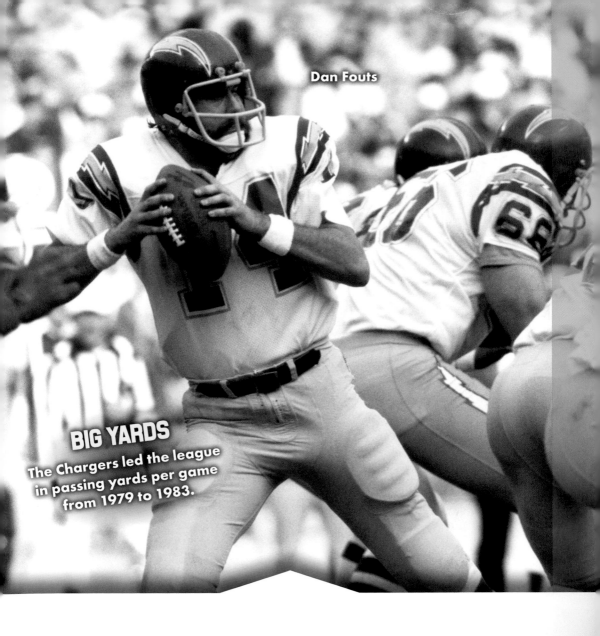

Dan Fouts

BIG YARDS
The Chargers led the league in passing yards per game from 1979 to 1983.

In the late 1970s, head coach Don Coryell developed a strong passing attack. His "Air Coryell" offense put up a lot of yards. It made quarterback Dan Fouts the top passer in the National Football League (NFL) at the time!

The Chargers have always called California home. But they have changed cities. They spent their first season in Los Angeles. Then they moved to San Diego.

For about 50 years, the Chargers have played at the open-air Qualcomm Stadium. But the team hopes to move to a new stadium soon.

QUALCOMM STADIUM

SAN DIEGO, CALIFORNIA

The Chargers joined the NFL in 1970. They play in the American Football **Conference** (AFC). They are part of the West **Division**.

The West Division includes the Denver Broncos, Kansas City Chiefs, and Oakland Raiders. The Chargers' main **rivals** are the Broncos and Raiders.

NFL DIVISIONS

AFC

AFC NORTH

BALTIMORE **RAVENS**

CINCINNATI **BENGALS**

CLEVELAND **BROWNS**

PITTSBURGH **STEELERS**

AFC EAST

BUFFALO **BILLS**

MIAMI **DOLPHINS**

PATRIOTS

NEW YORK **JETS**

AFC SOUTH

TEXANS

INDIANAPOLIS **COLTS**

JACKSONVILLE **JAGUARS**

TENNESSEE **TITANS**

AFC WEST

DENVER **BRONCOS**

CHIEFS

OAKLAND **RAIDERS**

SAN DIEGO **CHARGERS**

AFL RIVALS

The Chargers, Chiefs, Broncos, and Raiders were rivals even before they joined the NFL. They all played in the American Football League (AFL) together.

NFC

NFC NORTH

 CHICAGO
BEARS

 DETROIT
LIONS

 GREEN BAY
PACKERS

 MINNESOTA
VIKINGS

NFC EAST

 DALLAS
COWBOYS

 GIANTS

 PHILADELPHIA
EAGLES

 WASHINGTON
REDSKINS

NFC SOUTH

 **FALCONS**

 CAROLINA
PANTHERS

 NEW ORLEANS
SAINTS

BUCCANEERS

NFC WEST

 CARDINALS

 LOS ANGELES
RAMS

 SAN FRANCISCO
49ERS

 SEATTLE
SEAHAWKS

13

In 1960, the Chargers joined the AFL. They had a lot of success in the AFL. They made it to five title games. The Chargers won the championship for the 1963 season.

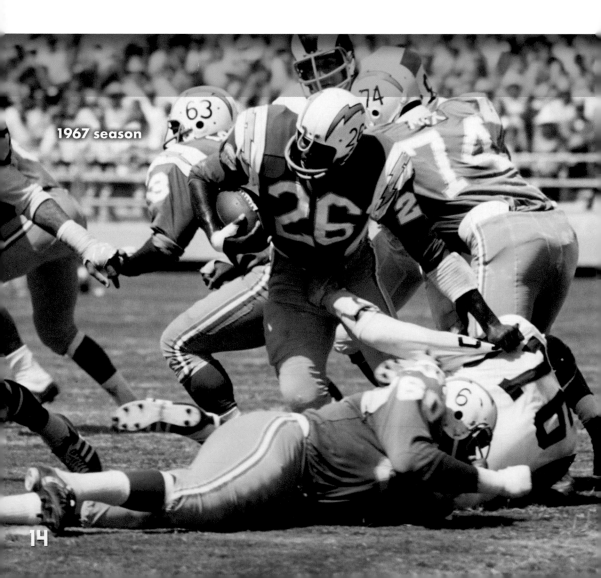

1967 season

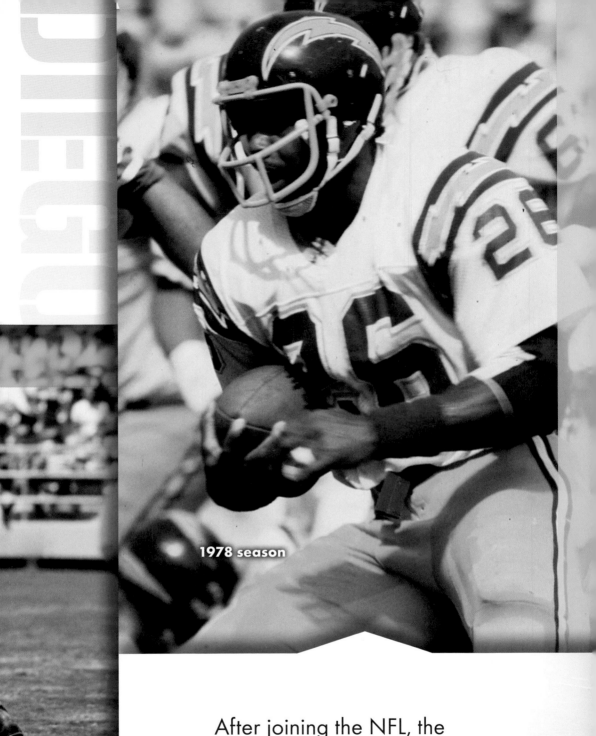

1978 season

After joining the NFL, the Chargers struggled. They did not have a winning season until 1978.

Don Coryell

Coryell became head coach in 1978. He turned the Chargers into a playoff team. Starting in 1979, they won three division titles in a row.

The team's best playoff run came in 1994. Bobby Ross was head coach. He led the team to **Super Bowl** 29.

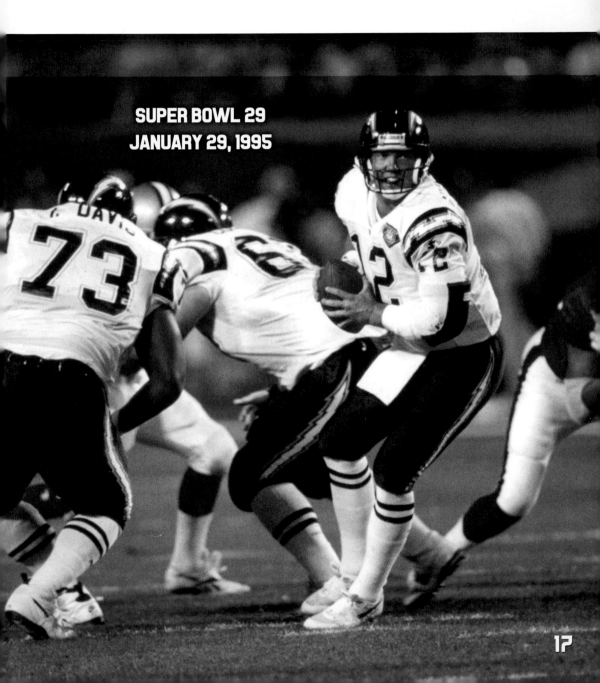

SUPER BOWL 29
JANUARY 29, 1995

CHARGERS
TIMELINE

1970

Joined the NFL

1960

Became part of the AFL (as the Los Angeles Chargers)

1961

Moved from Los Angeles to San Diego

1973

Drafted quarterback Dan Fouts

1964

Won the AFL Championship for the 1963 season, beating the Boston Patriots

51 FINAL SCORE **10**

1978

Hired head coach Don Coryell

1990

Drafted linebacker Junior Seau

2001

**Drafted running back
LaDainian Tomlinson**

1995

**Made it to Super Bowl 29, but
lost to the San Francisco 49ers**

26 FINAL SCORE **49**

2008

**Played in the AFC Championship
game for the 2007 season, but
lost to the New England Patriots**

12 FINAL SCORE **21**

Chargers fans have cheered on some great Hall-of-Famers. Lance Alworth was one of the league's best wide receivers during the 1960s.

Lance Alworth

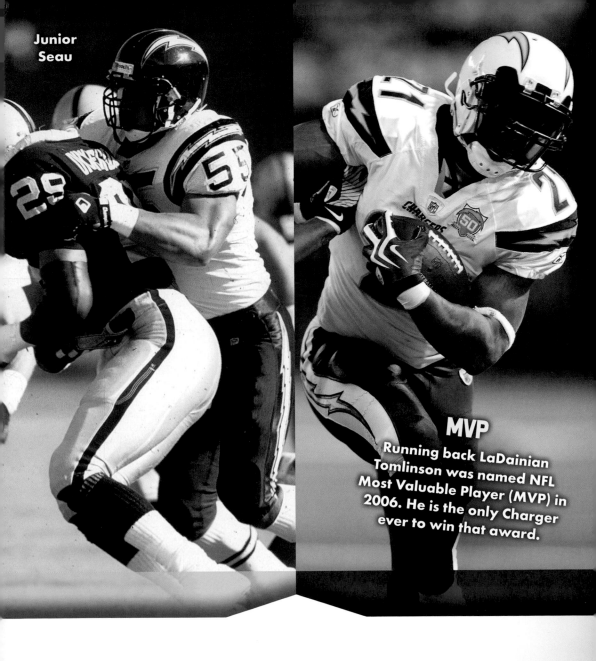

Junior
Seau

MVP
Running back LaDainian Tomlinson was named NFL Most Valuable Player (MVP) in 2006. He is the only Charger ever to win that award.

Fouts led the NFL in passing from 1979 to 1982. **Linebacker** Junior Seau was a tackling machine in the 1990s. He made the **Pro Bowl** twelve straight seasons from 1991 to 2002.

Rivers now leads the passing attack. One of his favorite targets has been **tight end** Antonio Gates. He is one of just two tight ends in NFL history to catch more than 100 touchdown passes.

Linebacker Manti Te'o is a rising star on **defense**. He had or helped with more than 200 tackles in his first three years in the league.

TEAM GREATS

LANCE ALWORTH
WIDE RECEIVER
1962-1970

DAN FOUTS
QUARTERBACK
1973-1987

JUNIOR SEAU
LINEBACKER
1990-2002

PASSING LEADER

Rivers led the league in passing in 2010. He recorded 4,710 passing yards.

LADAINIAN TOMLINSON
RUNNING BACK
2001-2009

ANTONIO GATES
TIGHT END
2003-PRESENT

PHILIP RIVERS
QUARTERBACK
2004-PRESENT

San Diego fans fill Qualcomm Stadium with blue and gold on game day. One of the craziest fans is Boltman. He dresses up like a lightning bolt to cheer the team on.

Boltman

Fans like to belt out "San Diego Super Chargers" at home games. This fight song has a fun disco beat.

In 2014, the Chargers decorated their stadium with new banners. These show their team history. They also include the retired jersey numbers.

Today, the team's young stars keep fans energized. Fans hope the next banner added will read: Super Bowl Champions!

MORE ABOUT THE CHARGERS

Team name:
San Diego Chargers

Team name explained:
**Named by a fan contest;
owner Barron Hilton also
liked yelling "Charge!"**

**Nicknames: The Bolts,
Super Chargers**

**Joined NFL: 1970
(AFL from 1960-1969)**

Conference: AFC

Division: West

**Main rivals: Denver Broncos,
Oakland Raiders**

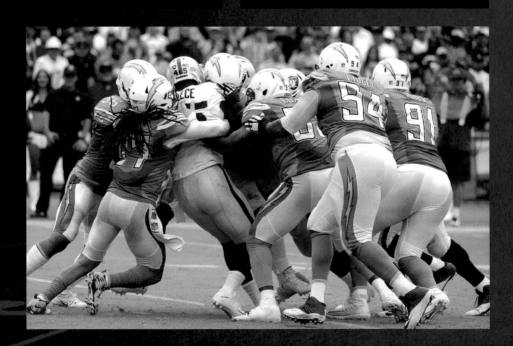

Hometown:
San Diego, California

Training camp location:
Chargers Park, San Diego, California

CALIFORNIA

N
W + E
S

SAN DIEGO

Home stadium name:
Qualcomm Stadium

Stadium opened: 1967

Seats in stadium: 70,561

Logo:
A yellow lightning bolt bordered in blue

Colors:
Navy blue, powder blue, white, gold

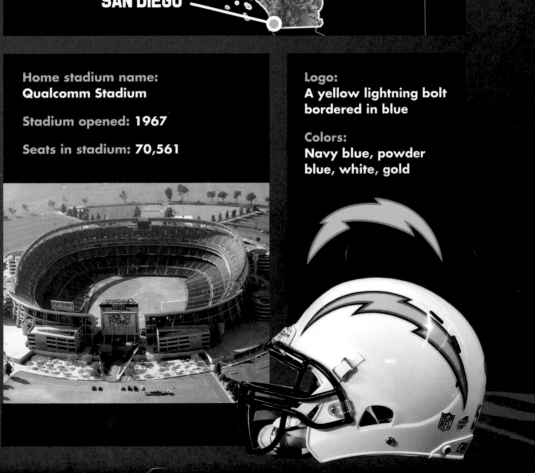

GLOSSARY

conference—a large grouping of sports teams that often play one another

defense—the group of players who try to stop the opposing team from scoring

division—a small grouping of sports teams that often play one another; usually there are several divisions of teams in a conference.

linebacker—a player on defense whose main job is to make tackles and stop passes; a linebacker stands just behind the defensive linemen.

offense—the group of players who try to move down the field and score

playoffs—the games played after the regular NFL season is over; playoff games determine which teams play in the Super Bowl.

Pro Bowl—an all-star game played after the regular season in which the best players in the NFL face one another

quarterback—a player on offense whose main job is to throw and hand off the ball

rivals—teams that are long-standing opponents

Super Bowl—the championship game for the NFL

tight end—a player on offense whose main jobs are to catch the ball and block for teammates

wide receiver—a player on offense whose main job is to catch passes from the quarterback

TO LEARN MORE

AT THE LIBRARY

Howell, Brian. *San Diego Chargers*. Mankato, Minn.: Child's World, 2015.

Whiting, Jim. *The Story of the San Diego Chargers*. Mankato, Minn.: Creative Education, 2014.

Wyner, Zach. *San Diego Chargers*. New York, N.Y.: AV2 by Weigl, 2015.

ON THE WEB

Learning more about the San Diego Chargers is as easy as 1, 2, 3.

1. Go to www.factsurfer.com.

2. Enter "San Diego Chargers" into the search box.

3. Click the "Surf" button and you will see a list of related web sites.

With factsurfer.com, finding more information is just a click away.

INDEX

The images in this book are reproduced through the courtesy of: Corbis, front cover (large, small), pp. 8-9, 10, 11 (top, bottom), 12-13, 21 (right), 22-23, 23 (middle), 24, 28; KC Alfred/ ZUMA Press/ Newscom, pp. 4-5; Paul Spinelli/ AP Images, pp. 5, 6-7 (top); Lenny Ignelzi/ AP Images, pp. 6-7 (bottom); David Eulitt/ MCT/ Newscom, p. 8; Deposit Photos/ Glow Images, pp. 12-13 (logos), 18-19 (logos), 28-29 (logos); NFL Photos/ AP Images, pp. 14-15, 22 (left, middle); Al Messerschmidt/ AP Images, pp. 15, 16, 18 (bottom); George Rose/ Getty Images, pp. 16-17; David Durochik/ AP Images, p. 18 (top); ZUMA Press/ Alamy, p. 19 (left); Photo Graphic Com/ Getty Images, p. 19 (right); Kevin Terrell/ AP Images, p. 21 (left); Four Seam Images/ AP Images, p. 22 (right); Paul Buck/ EPA/ Newscom, p. 23 (left, right); Denis Poroy/ AP Images, pp. 24-25; Tom Hauck/ AP Images, pp. 26-27; Nelvin C. Cepeda/ ZUMA Press/ Newscom, p. 27; f8grapher/ Alamy, p. 29 (stadium); Scott Boehm/ AP Images, p. 29 (helmet).